Hadith Al Kisa

The Event of the Cloak

(Colourful Children's Version)

By

R Mughal

ISBN-13: 978-1916416116

Dedication

"The first person to enter Paradise is Fatimah"

– The Holy Prophet, Muhammed.

I dedicate this book to Fatimah Zahra,
the daughter of Prophet Muhammed.
I pray this humble contribution will
earn me the honour of her intercession.

Foreword

Let our sincere intentions be to teach our children

such that they ponder

over their faith and their actions,

and what comes from it.

Acknowledgements

All praise is for Almighty God, without his providence

nothing can be conceived or achieved.

Thank you to everyone who played

an active part in supporting this venture.

My son Muhammed,

without you this would

not have been possible.

You are my best friend and my small taste of paradise.

Welcome to my house!

My name is Fatimah Zahra.

I have a special surprise for you.

I'm going to tell you about my father, Muhammad,

and the cloak called the Kisa.

Let's read on.

I'm really excited for you to learn about it, too.

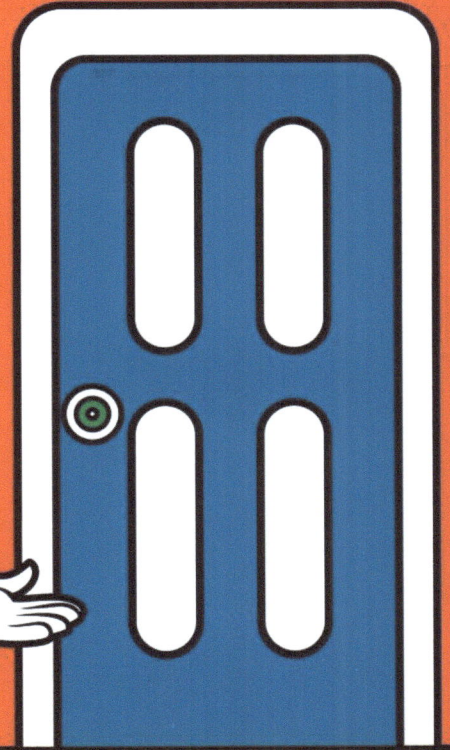

One day my father, Muhammad (the Messenger

of Allah),

came to my house.

"Assalaamu alayki, ya Fatimah," he said.

"Alaykas salaam," I replied, politely.

"Oh, Fatimah, please bring me the Kisa

and cover me with it," he requested.

After covering my father, I looked at his face.

It was glowing like the moon, so full of grace!

Then a little while later, my son, Hasan,

arrived.

"Assalaamu alayki, ya Umma."

"Alaykas salaam, my darling," I replied.

"I smell something beautiful and pure,

like the nice scent of my grandfather...for sure,"

said Hasan, with a big smile.

So, Hasan joined my father under the Kisa.

Soon after, my son, Hussayn, arrived.

"Assalaamu alayki, ya Umma."

"Alaykas salaam, my darling," I replied.

"I smell something beautiful and pure, like the nice scent of my grandfather...for sure," said Hussayn, with a big smile.

So Hussayn too, joined my father under the Kisa.

Then came Ali, my husband and my father's cousin.

"Assalaamu alayki, o daughter of the Messenger of Allah."

"Alaykas salaam, Ameerul Mu'mineen," I replied.

"I smell something beautiful and pure,

like the nice scent of my cousin

...for sure," said Ali, with a big smile.

So, Ali too, joined my father under the Kisa.

I then peered under the cloak.

"Assalaamu alaykum, my father.

Can I please join you all under the Kisa?"

"Yes, of course, my darling.

YOU are a part of me, Fatimah," he replied.

My father, Muhammad, was so happy,

and being the Messenger, he spoke with Allah!

"O Allah, my Ahlul Bayt are under this special cloak,

please continue keeping them safe and purified."

"O Muhammed, I made everything

in the heavens and the earth,

for you Five Ahlul Kisa!" replied Almighty Allah.

The angel Jibraeel heard Allah's voice and asked,

"Who are these special five people under the Kisa?"

"They are the family of Fatimah:

Her father, Muhammad;

Her husband, Ali;

And her sons, Hasan and Hussayn," replied Allah.

They are the Ahlul Bayt, The Pure Ones.

Fatimah Muhammed
Ali Hasan Hussayn

Jibraeel was so excited and quickly

rushed to Fatimah's house.

He too wanted to join the Ahlul Bayt.

And he too, sat under the Kisa!

"I wonder what this means...," said

Ali Ameerul Mu'mineen.

"Why did our family gather like this

under this cloak, the Kisa?" he asked.

"Allah brought us together to make us

the Ahlul Bayt, The Pure Ones," replied

Muhammad.

"Remembering this event has a special power!

It takes away sadness and loneliness.

Ask Allah for anything you wish!

Allah will send his angels from heaven to pray

for you!"

"WOW, how wonderful!" replied

Ali Ameerul Mu'mineen.

"Now that is a special gift from Almighty Allah!

What an amazing Lord!"

So, there you are Children!

What started with my father and the Kisa,

Made us The Pure Ones because of

what was said by Almighty Allah:

إِنَّمَا يُرِيدُ اللَّهُ لِيُذْهِبَ عَنكُمُ الرِّجْسَ أَهْلَ الْبَيْتِ وَيُطَهِّرَكُمْ تَطْهِيرًا

(33:33)

("Inna Maa yuree dul Allahu Li yudhhibah an kum rijsa Ahlu Bayti
wayou Tahhira kum Tat heeraa")

"Indeed Allah desires to repel all impurity from you,

O People of the Household, and purify you with a thorough

purification." *(Tanzil.net Translation by Qarai)*

Please share this book

with all your family and friends!

@FourteenFiveBooks

Word List:

Ahlul-Bayt - Term to describe the "People of the House" or "Family of the House". In this amazing event, it shows us who these people are

Ahlul Kisa – People of the Cloak or Blanket

Ameerul Mu'mineen – The title given to Ali for being the best of leaders for all the faithful Muslims

Jibraeel – Arabic name for the Angel Gabriel

Kisa – The Special Blanket or Cloak that was used by Muhammed

Messenger of Allah – Muhammed, who passed on the message directly from Almighty Allah to everyone else

Prophet - a person who is granted a special power by God that allows him to talk directly to God

33:33 - This refers to the Surah (chapter) and Verse number in the holy book, the glorious Quran. Give it a try and see if you can find it next time

Umma - Arabic word which means mother

FOURTEEN FIVE BOOKS

COLOURFUL ISLAMIC NARRATIONS FOR LITTLE MONSTERS

www.ingramcontent.com/pod-product-compliance
Lightning Source LLC
Chambersburg PA
CBHW041526070426
42452CB00036B/26